Pooches

Milly Brown

summersdale

POOCHES

Summersdale Publishers Ltd
46 West Street
Chichester
West Sussex
PO19 1RP
UK

www.summersdale.com

Printed and bound by Tien Wah Press, Singapore.

All images © Shutterstock

ISBN: 1-84024-599-9
ISBN 13: 978-1-84024-599-8

For Freddie

They said size zero was in, but this is just ridiculous!

Fashion is not what you wear – it's a way of life.

So the plastic box floats. Very funny. Can you rescue me now?

I don't just think I'm cool; I *know* I'm cool.

She's my third wife. I think she's the one.

Catalogue
modelling isn't
my full-time job.

Do you come here often?

Excuse me...
HELP!

It really is the best way to chase next door's cat.

Here I come to save the day!

Happy Easter
– do I look
happy?!

It's a Jane Austen adaptation; I'm playing the baby.

He hasn't proposed yet, but there's no harm in hoping!

Please don't make me go... the other dogs tease me.

If I concentrate
hard enough
maybe my butt
will get smaller.

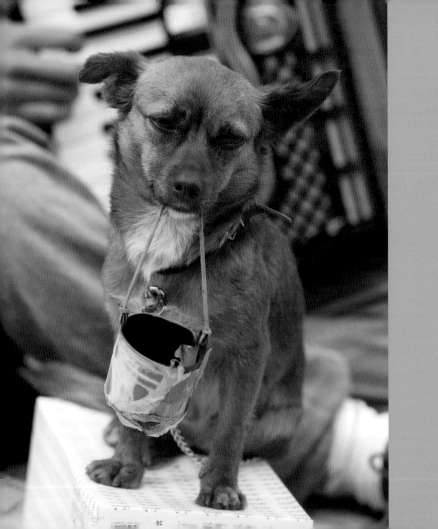

I have a crash pad in the city and a pile of bricks in the country. I just do this for fun.

Campfire
Marshmallows
Milwaukee, Wis., Cambridge, Mass.
For Baking Topping

I'm not cute.
I'm mean.

With house prices rising it's really important to have a paw on the property ladder.

I'll discuss it with you in a minute, I'm just chewing things over.

Why did we move here? I don't even like green.

Kill me.
Just kill
me now.

Note to self;
never fall asleep
with curlers in...

Well, it's definitely better than last year's office party, eh boys?

Is there a prize
at Crufts for
being absolutely
adorable?

That's the thing about getting older – another day, another wrinkle. Isn't that right ladies?

I feel so exposed, and yet, so free.

A moment
on the lips.
A lifetime on
the hips.

Yoga has changed my life. I feel like a puppy again!

Well, there was this one time we climbed Everest...

Being rich has its advantages: I don't walk anywhere.

I love shopping,
makeovers and
really long walks,
if you're interested,
give me a call!

If I'm really good can I ride up front with you?

Anyone for fajitas?

I asked the hairdresser for strawberry blonde; I'm taking them to court.

When you look
this good, you
can be as bad
as you like.

Quotable Dogs

£5.99

ISBN: 1-84024-537-9
ISBN: 978-1-84024-537-0

No matter how little money and how few possessions you own, having a dog makes you rich.

Louis Sabin

A stunning photographic book with quotes about canines, this delightful celebration of your best friend and loyal companion is a pooch of a gift for every dog-lover.

Quotable Cats

£5.99

ISBN: 1-84024-536-0
ISBN: 978-1-84024-536-3

Thousands of years ago, cats were worshipped as gods. Cats have never forgotten this.

Anonymous

A beautiful photographic book with quotes about cats, this delightful celebration of the world's favourite furry friend is the purrfect gift for every cat-lover.

www.summersdale.com